# Born Guilty?

## A Southern Baptist
## View of Original Sin

*by*
*Adam Harwood, Ph.D.*

ISBN978-1-939283-02-3

Printed in the United States.

Jacket and Interior design—Debbie Patrick, Vision Run www.visionrun.com

Free Church Press
P. O. Box Box 1075
Carrollton, GA 30112

# Introduction

Bible-believing Christians agree that people are sinners in need of God's grace. Also, most Christians agree that Adam's sin in the garden had devastating consequences for the human race. But Christians disagree on the precise nature of our inheritance from Adam. Do we receive from Adam a sinful nature or Adam's guilt? At first glance, these choices appear to be identical. But these phrases represent different views. The differences emerge when questions are explored, such as: Did Adam sin alone or did the human race sin with him? Did God enter with Adam into a covenant, which is not mentioned in the Bible? Are all people born guilty and condemned by God due to Adam's sin? Or do individuals become guilty and condemned when they personally attain moral capability and commit their own sin? Questions like these are usually discussed among Christians under the broad rubric of "Original Sin."

In the following pages, I will focus on one clarifying question: Who is guilty of Adam's sin? As I proceed, the reader will recognize that only two answers to this question exist. We will examine the question in light of Scripture, theology, and history. My goal is for the reader to understand the significance of the question and the need for a biblical answer. Finally, I will point out the implications for my own denomination–The Southern Baptist Convention.

## Two Basic Views

*Who is guilty of Adam's sin? Christians differ when answering this question. The first view answers: Adam. Only Adam is guilty of Adam's sin. The reason? According to the Bible, God judges people for their own sins. Because all people are a descendant of Adam, sin comes naturally. All are born in a fallen environment with an inescapable inclination toward sin and a body subject to death. From our first moment of life, we are soaked in sin. As David cried, "Surely I was sinful at birth, sinful from the time my mother conceived me" (Ps 51:5 NIV). Upon attaining the knowledge of good and evil (Deut 1:39; Isa 7:15–16), individuals are judged by God for their own thoughts, attitudes, and actions. Sin entered the world through Adam's sin; death and condemnation followed. But God judges only Adam to be guilty for his sin. Names for this view include inherited inclination or what some call "original death."[1] In this view, we're not guilty of Adam's sin. Rather, we begin life with an inclination toward sin. Physical death can occur prior to personal transgression of the law. But we become transgressors who are guilty and under condemnation for our own sin only when we attain moral capability and first commit—knowingly commit—a sinful thought, attitude, or action. This is the inherited sinful nature view, the view I hold and for which I argue throughout this brief presentation.[2]*

A second view answers the question this way: Adam and his descendants are guilty of Adam's sin (Jesus, of course, is exempted). Every person is guilty of Adam's sin. Why? Because God judges people for their own sins–and for the guilt of Adam's sin. Notice that both views say God judges people for their own sins. The difference is the second view includes the guilt of Adam's sin and thus endorses the views held by Catholics and some Protestants beginning with Augustine in the fourth century. Augustine (AD 354–430) was an extremely influential Roman Catholic Bishop in North Africa. He held a view we call "natural headship." In his later writings, Augustine said all people are guilty of Adam's sin because they were present with him physically or seminally when he sinned. Though John Calvin was a

Protestant, he agreed with Augustine in general but viewed Adam as our representative head who acted on behalf of humanity in the garden. Many Reformed Christians agree with Calvin. Their view is usually called "Federal Headship." Moreover, in the seventeenth century, a group of Protestant Christians embraced what's called "Covenant Theology." They point to a covenant of works between Adam and God, which Adam transgressed for humanity when he sinned. Wayne Grudem, a contemporary Calvinist and Covenant theologian, explains: "As our representative, Adam sinned, and God counted us guilty as well as Adam."[3] Thus, they believe that in addition to a sinful nature all people inherit from Adam, all people inherit the guilt of Adam's sin as well. This is the inherited guilt view.

Hence, while some offer qualifications to their position, when the question is asked, "Who is guilty of Adam's sin?" only two answers exist: only Adam or Adam and all humanity. The inherited sinful nature view says all people inherit from Adam sin and mortality. The inherited guilt view affirms those but includes the inheritance of guilt. Both are orthodox positions. Nevertheless, I will argue that the inherited sinful nature view finds stronger support biblically, theologically, and historically (especially for Southern Baptists).

Understanding there are two possible Christian answers to our question, which both depend upon the Scripture, let's consider what is regarded widely as the most important biblical text when considering the guilt of Adam's sin, Romans 5:12–21.

## The Significance of Context

Before examining the actual text, a proper method for interpreting Scripture requires us to consider its context. What were Paul's earlier points leading up to our passage?

After greeting the saints in Rome, Paul announces his thesis (1:16–17). The righteousness of God is by faith; the just will live by faith in Jesus Christ. In 1:18–3:20, Paul argues that God justly judges all sinners. Creation and conscience declare the existence of the creator and law–giver. But Jew and Gentile have defied God by worshipping created things. Both Jew and Gentile have God's law, whether it is inscribed on stone or inscribed on their hearts. Because both Jew and Gentile have known of God's existence and God's law yet defied Him by their actions, they are under sin (3:9). Works of the law will not bring justification but, knowledge of sin comes through the law (3:20).

Romans 3:21 begins a presentation of the Good News. The Old Testament law and prophets testify: Righteousness comes apart from the law through faith in Jesus Christ for all who believe. God is God of both Jews and Gentiles (3:29). In chapter 4, God justifies people, both Jew and Gentile, like He justified Abraham: by faith. Those who believe in Jesus, who died for our sins and was raised for our justification, will be counted as righteous before God (4:24–25).

In 5:1–2, we've been justified by faith and have peace with God through Christ. And we access this grace through Christ by faith. Those given the Holy Spirit can hope in their suffering because of God's work in them (vv. 3–5). Christ died for "the weak" and "ungodly," people who were "still sinners" (vv. 6–8). In verse 1, we're justified by faith; in verse 9, we're justified by His blood. In verses 9–11, we'll be saved from wrath and reconciled to God through Jesus. Or, as N. T. Wright outlines it:

**The problem of sin and death (1:18–3:20)**

**The solution of justification and life (3:21–5:11)**[4]

## Romans 5:12–21

Now that we have rehearsed the context leading up to our key passage, note Paul's words in Romans 5:12–21:

**12** Therefore, just as sin came into the world through one man, and death through sin, and so death spread to all men *because all sinned— 13 for sin indeed was in the world before the law was given, but sin is not counted where there is no law. 14 Yet death reigned from Adam to Moses, even over those whose sinning was not like the transgression of Adam, who was a type of the one who was to come.*

*15 But the free gift is not like the trespass. For if many died through one man's trespass, much more have the grace of God and the free gift by the grace of that one man Jesus Christ abounded for many. 16 And the free gift is not like the result of that one man's sin. For the judgment following one trespass brought condemnation, but the free gift following many trespasses brought justification. 17 For if, because of one man's trespass, death reigned through that one man, much more will those who receive the abundance of grace and the free gift of righteousness reign in life through the one man Jesus Christ.*

*18 Therefore, as one trespass led to condemnation for all men, so one act of righteousness leads to justification and life for all men. 19 For as by the one man's disobedience the many were made sinners, so by the one man's obedience the many will be made righteous. 20 Now the law came in to increase the trespass, but where sin increased, grace abounded all the more, 21 so that, as sin reigned in death, grace also might reign through righteousness leading to eternal life through Jesus Christ our Lord.[5]*

## What Resulted from Adam's Sin?

*Explaining every word of Rom 5:12–21 would exceed our available space and would be unnecessary. Why? There is agreement on most of the text. For that reason, I'll highlight only the differences. According to the text, what resulted from Adam's sin?*

*Adam's disobedience in the garden ushered into the world sin, death, and condemnation (Greek: hamartia, thanatos, and katakrima respectively). Verse 12 says: "Therefore, just as sin (hamartia) came into the world through one man, and death (thanantos) through sin, and so death spread to all men because all sinned—."*

### Sin Entered the World

*Notice in verse 12 that something came into the world. Something not present in the beginning later came into the world. What does the text say? Sin. Sin came into God's world. It was an intruder in God's good creation. Did a sinful nature or sinful actions enter the world? Both. Sin entered the world through Adam's one "trespass" (paraptōmatos, v. 18) or "disobedience" (parakoōs, v. 19). Joseph Fitzmyer calls sin "the personified malevolent force...hostile to God and alienating human beings from him."[6] How did sin come into the world? Verse 12 says, "through one man." When he fell (Genesis 3), Adam became the portal for this intruder called sin.*

### Death Spread to All Men

*Returning to verse 12: "Therefore, just as sin came into the world through one man, and death through sin, and so death spread to all men because all sinned—." Death entered the world through sin. It wasn't a creation of God but the consequence of Adam's sin. Death "reigned" through Adam (v. 17). The Good News is that before establishing His world, God planned for the entrance of sin, death, and condemnation by providing the atoning sacrifice for our sin in the life, death, and resurrection of Christ.*

### Because All Sinned

*Examine the simple chart and observe how Christian interpretations diverged from the clear declaration of the Apostle Paul:*

| Romans 5:12 | Augustinian Inherited Guilt | Covenant Theology's Inherited Guilt |
|---|---|---|
| Therefore, just as sin came into the world through one man and death through sin and so death spread to all men... | | |
| because all sinned. | in whom all sinned. | because all sinned (in Adam). |

*Notice that the text says neither "in whom all sinned" (the Augustinian view) nor "because all sinned in Adam" (the Covenant Theology view). The text simply says: "death spread to all men because all sinned." The phrase "because all sinned" is used by the following English versions of the Bible: ESV, HCSB, NASB, NIV, NKJV, NET, and other translations. What exactly did Paul mean by these words? The United Bible Societies'* A Translator's Handbook on Paul's Letter to the Romans *comments on Rom 5:12:*

> Paul indicates that Adam sinned, and as a result of his sin death came into the human race. However, it is important to realize that Paul does not make men guilty of Adam's sin or indicate that all men die because of the sin of Adam. Paul says rather that death spread to the whole human race, because all men sinned.[7]

*Augustine misread Rom 5:12 by relying on Old Latin and Vulgate translations[8] or the influence of western theologians. In either case, Augustine's misinterpretation has shaped the Christian tradition. Roman Catholic scholar Joseph Fitzmyer explains that the doctrine of original sin (the view that all people inherit both the sin and guilt of Adam) is not an explicit teaching of Paul. Rather, the doctrine was developed from Augustine's later writings and solidified through the 16th Council of Carthage, the 2nd Council of Orange, and the Tridentine Council. But, Fitzmyer explains, Paul did not teach the doctrine of original sin.[9]*

*The Covenant Theology view is affirmed by John Murray, Wayne Grudem, and Michael Horton. In 1959, Murray published* The Imputation of Adam's Sin, *a biblical–historical examination of Rom 5:12–21. Murray argues that death came to all people because all sinned in Adam. In this way, God counts all people guilty because of Adam's sin. But there are two great weaknesses in this Covenant interpretation. First, the Bible never says "all sinned in Adam." Covenant Theologians insist on a view not required by the text. Second, their interpretation depends on two theological constructs not explicitly stated in Scripture: the covenant of redemption (which depends upon the Calvinistic doctrine of unconditional election and a pact among the persons of the Trinity) and the covenant of works (between God and Adam).[10] Once again, a critique is simple: these covenants are not in the Bible.*

*Jack MacGorman served for half a century at Southwestern Baptist Theological Seminary (SWBTS) in Fort Worth, Texas and is now Distinguished Professor Emeritus of New Testament. MacGorman makes this point about the covenant of works: "It has influenced greatly the churches of the Reformed tradition. However, there is not one shred of evidence in the Bible that God ever entered into such a covenant with Adam. The theory was born in Europe, not Eden."[11]*

*Verse 14 explains that "Adam...was a type of the one to come." Adam is a type of Christ. Many Old Testament characters can be viewed as a type (or foreshadowing) of Christ but this verse should remove any doubt. Adam is a type of Christ. Also, Paul contrasts the two figures. In the case of Adam:*

> *v. 18, "Therefore, as one trespass led to condemnation for all men..."*

> *v. 19, "For as by the one man's disobedience the many were made sinners..."*

*What is Paul's point in this Adam–Christ parallel? Covenant Theologians say there are two heads of humanity. Adam imputes guilt to all people; Christ imputes righteousness to the elect. Is that Paul's meaning in Romans 5?*

*Does the text say that Adam's guilt and condemnation are imputed to all people? Or does it say that sin enters the world, death enters through sin, and death spreads because all sinned? In this way, Adam's "one trespass led to condemnation for all men" (v. 17). Paul's point in Rom 1:18–3:20 is that all people are individually accountable to God and condemned only when they deny the existence of God and transgress His law. People become condemned because of their actions.*

*The inherited guilt view presses the Adam-Christ parallel then rejects the implications for the view. If guilt and condemnation are imputed to all people through Adam, then justification and life are imputed to all people through Christ (v. 19). Both views reject Universalism as Paul's intended meaning. There are other orthodox interpretations of the passage. Millard Erickson affirms "conditional imputation."[12] Just as we must ratify the work of Christ in our life by personally repenting of sin and believing in Christ, so we must personally ratify the work of Adam in our life by personally and knowingly committing a sinful act. In this way, neither Universalism nor imputed guilt are necessary conclusions for Rom 5:12–21.*

### What do the Bible, theology, and history say about Adam's guilt and whether God holds people accountable for their own sin or the sin of Adam?

*It is unwise to build a theological system on a single biblical passage, such as Rom 5:12–21. In order to guard against "eisegesis" (reading our theological pre-commitments into a biblical text), I will broaden our investigation to the nature of accountability to God and test the inherited sinful nature view biblically, historically, and theologically. First, a brief survey of the Bible will answer this question: For what does God hold people accountable and under condemnation, their own sin or the sin of Adam? Second, the view will be tested against the doctrine of general revelation. Third, the view will find support in a brief survey of church and Baptist history.*

## What the Bible teaches about accountability and Adam's sin

Let's affirm what the Bible affirms on particular matters and resist any theological system—even our own—which demands we affirm more than the Bible clearly teaches on the matter. Throughout the Bible, people give an account to God. He judges their sinful thoughts, attitudes, and actions—with no mention of Adam's guilt.

- Genesis 3: God judges the serpent, Adam, and Eve for their own sins. Because of Adam's sin, the ground is cursed and our bodies return to dust (vv. 17–19). But there is no mention that future generations would be judged guilty or personally held accountable for Adam's sin.

- Genesis 4: God judges Cain for killing Abel—no mention of Adam's guilt.

- Genesis 6: God judges humanity minus one family. Why? "The Lord saw that the wickedness of man was great in the earth, and that every intention of the thoughts of his heart was only evil continually" (v. 5)—no mention of Adam's guilt.

- Genesis 11: God judges tower–builders.

- Genesis 19: God judges Sodom and Gomorrah because of sexual sin.

- Genesis 19: God judges Lot's wife for looking back.

- Exodus 12: God judges the firstborn to deliver His people.

- Exodus 32: God judges the Israelites for their idolatry at the foot of Mt. Sinai.

- Leviticus 10: God judges Nadab and Abihu for offering "strange fire" (v. 1 KJV).

- Numbers 14: God judges the older generation of Israelites for believing the ten spies rather than God—but no mention of Adam's guilt.

- Joshua 7: God judges Achan and his family because he stole from God and thought God couldn't see through dirt.

- 1 Samuel 3: God judges Eli's sons for dishonoring the Temple.

- *1 Samuel 13: God judges Saul—ending his kingdom—because he didn't keep God's command (v. 13).*

- *2 Samuel 12: God judges David's adultery and murder. His baby son dies and his family declines—but there is no mention of Adam's guilt.*

- *Psalm 62:12: the Lord "will render to a man according to his work."*

- *Proverbs 24:12: we hear the question, Will the Lord "not repay man according to his work?"*

*When considering the prophets, Ezekiel indicates that neither righteousness nor wickedness is shared from father to son. God judges the one who sins (18:20). Hosea is the only prophet to mention Adam. In 6:7, he writes of Israel and Judah: "But like Adam they transgressed the covenant." All of the prophets, major and minor, address the sinful thoughts, attitudes, and actions of individuals or nations. Typically, God's people have broken covenant with the Lord by their idolatry, injustice, and/or empty religion. However, none of the prophets mention Adam's guilt.*

*After surveying the Old Testament, we may confidently conclude that no prophet mentions Adam's guilt or our inheriting his guilt from Eden's tragedy. For them, our moral accountability to God concerns our personal failures of injustice and idolatry among a host of other immoral behaviors.*

*Now let's consider passages from the New Testament pertaining to our moral accountability to God:*

- *Matthew 12: Jesus says "on the day of judgment people will give account for every careless word they speak, for by your words you will be justified, and by your words you will be condemned" (vv. 36b–37).[13] (emphasis added.)*

- *Mark 7: Jesus explains: "What comes out of a person is what defiles him. For from within, out of the heart of man, come evil thoughts, sexual immorality, theft, murder, adultery, coveting, wickedness, deceit, sensuality, envy, slander, pride, foolishness. All these evil things come from within, and they defile a person" (vv. 20–23). Jesus failed to mention Adam's guilt. Instead, each person is defiled by his own sinful thoughts, attitudes, and actions.*

- *Romans 1: Paul argues "the wrath of God is revealed from heaven against all ungodliness and unrighteousness of men" (v. 18). Does Paul mention Adam's guilt? When indicting humanity for sin, Paul could have declared universal guilt because of Adam's sin. Instead, he lists ungodly and unrighteous actions, including suppressing the truth (v. 18), failing to honor God (v. 21), claiming to be wise (v. 22), and worshipping created things rather than the creator (vv. 23 and 25). The result? God gave them up to their passions (v. 26).*

- *Romans 2: Paul clearly states people will be judged for their deeds (v. 6).*

- *1 Peter 1:17: Peter says we call on a "Father who judges impartially according to each one's deeds."*

- *James 1: James notes the progression of personal responsibility. A person "is lured and enticed by his own desire." Then desire conceives and "gives birth to sin, and sin when it is fully grown brings forth death" (vv. 14–15).*

- *Revelation 20:12: in John's vision of judgment at the great white throne, "the dead were judged by what was written in the books, according to what they had done."*

*While I could have added many more Scriptures to this brief survey, I remain convinced the inherited sinful nature view better accounts for the Bible's teachings on the nature of God's judgment than the view which insists Adam's guilt is imputed to every human being. Some may suggest I isolated the verses from their respective contexts and consequently "eisegeted" them (i.e. read into the texts my own personal meaning). I challenge readers to employ the same method—a plain reading of Scripture using standard grammatical and historical tools—and judge whether I have read my own personal meaning into the Bible. I remain confident what will be found: God's judgment and wrath falls on people for their own sins, not the sin of Adam. I fully embrace the*

*Reformers' cry of Sola Scriptura (Scripture alone settles the issue) and therefore look to the words of Moses, David, Solomon, all of the prophets, Paul, Peter, James, John, and Jesus. While quoting what Reformed theologians have to say about the passages may inform us historically, we can never, ever substitute the theology of men for the Word of God.*

### What systematic theology teaches about accountability and Adam's sin

God reveals His existence and His law through creation and conscience (Rom 1:19–20; 2:15). And God will hold people accountable for this knowledge. Systematic theologians refer to this as general revelation. Romans 1:20 declares that people are "without excuse." Some people may claim God doesn't exist, but they know He exists. They try to suppress that truth and fail to worship Him (vv. 18 and 21), but the Creator reveals His existence through creation. Also, the law–giver reveals His law through the human conscience. Paul argues in Romans 2 that Jews and Gentiles are sinners. Then, he anticipates an objection: Can the Gentiles be considered innocent of law–breaking since they were not given the law of Moses? No, because their conscience demonstrates that God's law is written on their hearts (Rom 2:14–15). Knowing an action violates God's law doesn't prevent one from committing the action. But knowing this and doing it anyway brings God's wrath. That is the bad news which makes the gospel such good news.

The result? Every person who recognizes the existence of a creator and law–giver is accountable to that creator and law–giver, which excludes infants and the mentally incompetent. Who would interpret Romans 1–2 in such a way? John Piper. Consider his reply when asked: "What happens to infants who die?" Piper doesn't begin his answer with Adam's guilt; he begins with Romans 1 and 2. Piper says:

*I think they're all saved. In other words, I don't buy the principle that says that children born into "covenant families" are secure, and children born into "non-covenant families" aren't. I don't go there.*

*My reason for thinking they're all saved is because of the principle in Romans 1 where Paul argues that all people know God, and they are "without excuse" because they do not honor him or glorify him as God.*

*His argument is that they are without excuse because they know things, as though accountability in the presence of God at the Last Judgment will be based, at least partly, on whether they had access to necessary knowledge.*

*And God says they've all got access to knowledge, because they can look at the things he has made and see his power and deity. But they suppress that knowledge instead of submitting to it, therefore they're all condemned.*

*So I ask the question: OK, is the principle being raised there that, if you don't have access to the knowledge that causes you to be held accountable, therefore you will not be accountable? And I think that's the case.*

*I think babies and imbeciles—that is, those with profound mental disabilities—don't have access to the knowledge that they will be called to account for. Therefore, somehow in some way, God, through Christ, covers these people.*

*So that, in a nutshell, is why I think all children who die in infancy are elect and will be, through Jesus Christ, saved in ways that I may not know how, as God honors this principle of accountability.[14]*

I am not suggesting that John Piper denies inherited guilt. He affirms inherited guilt. My point is this: When asked about the eternal destiny of infants, Piper appeals to Romans 1–2 to explain that infants and the mentally incompetent are not accountable to God. Precisely! If that is the case, then in what way are they ever guilty of Adam's sin?

I understand Piper affirms the atoning work of Christ covers those who die in this unaccountable state. But so do we. The dif-

ference is this: *We don't insist they are guilty of Adam's sin. Such
an affirmation creates a problem. Why? Guilty people must repent of their sin and believe in Jesus. Because I don't add Adam's
sin and guilt, I don't insist the infants are guilty. Instead, they
are sin-stained, but not guilty. This condition could be covered
by a passive application of the atonement. But when one insists
that they are guilty, then they should repent and believe. Piper
acknowledged this in a footnote of his recent book,* Jesus: The
Only Way to God: Must You Hear the Gospel to be Saved? *How does
Piper think the work of Christ is received by these unaccountable
people? He speculates that infants who die will mature after death
and confess Christ.*[15]

Perhaps Piper's speculation regarding post-mortem confessions
of Christ results from his commitment to inherited guilt. When
Piper allowed Romans 1 and 2 to guide his thinking, he regarded
infants to be not yet accountable to God. But upon affirming this
extra-biblical position called inherited guilt, his view of infant salvation morphs into post-mortem confessions of Christ. Inherited
guilt is problematic because it requires one to say more than the
Bible plainly reveals about the time of accountability and guilt.

When arguing that Jews and Gentiles are guilty before God
(Romans 1–2), Paul doesn't point to Adam's sin. Instead, he
points to their willful rejection of their Creator and transgression
of the His law—with no mention of Adam's guilt.

### What historical theology teaches about accountability and Adam's sin

In A Theology for the Church, *Stan Norman writes: "First, the
Augustinian doctrine of original sin has exerted profound influence upon the theology of the church. Since his time, theologians
have affirmed, rejected, or modified the Augustinian position."
Norman adds: "Second, no consensus exists within Christianity
on the effects of sin upon humanity."*[16] *Below are some theologians who have denied inherited guilt.*

### · Eastern Tradition

**John Chrysostom** (374–407), known as "Golden Mouth" for his oratorical skill, is regarded as one of the most significant preachers in the first thousand years of Christian history. He wrote: "We do baptize infants, although they are not guilty of any sins."[17]

**Gregory of Nyssa** (ca. 335–394) was a leading participant at the Council of Constantinople (381). In On Infants' Early Deaths, he addresses the spiritual condition of infants. Gregory considers them to be neither good nor bad; infants who died would be with God because their souls had never been corrupted by their own sinful actions.[18]

### · Western Tradition

Eastern theologians were not alone in rejecting—at least failing to appeal to—inherited guilt. **Tertullian** (ca. 145–ca. 220) mentions that infant souls are unclean in Adam (consistent with inherited sinful nature view). And he questions why there was a rush to baptize them. Consider: those who taught inherited guilt insisted on infant baptism, wrongly assuming that water baptism cleaned the infants of Adam's guilt. Tertullian referred to the souls of infants as "innocent" and he differentiated between infants and children based upon their capability to commit sin.[19] Eric Osborne concludes, "While Tertullian displays the origins of the idea, one cannot attribute the later doctrine of original sin to him."[20]

### · Reformers

Inherited guilt was rejected by one of the **Magisterial Reformers, Ulrich Zwingli** (1484–1531). Like Martin Luther, Zwingli rejected the Augustinian notion that baptism removed the guilt of original sin. Zwingli admitted he previously held the view. He wrote: "We also believed that the water of baptism cleansed children from a sin that they never had, and that without it they would be damned. All these beliefs were erroneous, as we shall see later." Zwingli affirmed Adam's unity with humanity and sin's devastating *effects upon humanity. But he calls original sin a "sin that they never had."*

*Luther attacked Zwingli's position as Pelagian. Zwingli defended his view of original sin by asking: "For what could be said more briefly and plainly than that original sin is not sin but disease, and that the children of Christians are not condemned to eternal punishment on account of that disease?" Zwingli also distinguished between disease and sin. Disease refers to the "original contamination of man," "defect of humanity," or "the defect of a corrupted nature." Adam's fault brought this to every person (Rom 5:14). Sin, however, "implies guilt, and guilt comes from a transgression or a trespass on the part of one who designedly perpetrates a deed." Zwingli was unwilling to state that the inheritance from Adam should be called "sin" because Zwingli denied that the inheritance from Adam involves "guilt," which implies a sinful deed.[21]*

**Pilgram Marpeck** *(1495–1556) was an Anabaptist Reformer who, like Zwingli, also had to refute the charge of Pelagianism. Marpeck wrote:*

> *Our witness is that for children neither inherited nor actual sin counts before God because a child remains in ignorance and in created simplicity until it grows up into understanding and the inheritance is realized in and through it. Before that, sin has no damning effect; neither inherited nor actual sin is counted against a child before God. . . . When children come to a knowledge of good and evil, that is, when they reach understanding, then the inheritance which leads to damnation becomes effective in them. Then inherited sin becomes inheritable.[22]*

### • Baptists

*Affirmations of inherited sinful nature (or denials of inherited guilt) haven't been universal in Christian history but they have been frequent. This was demonstrated by theologians of both the Eastern and Western traditions and the Magisterial* and Anabaptist Reformers. The view has been affirmed frequently among Baptists. Consider as examples: a 400-year old confession of a Baptist "founder," 100 years of theology at Southwestern Baptist Theological Seminary (SWBTS), statements from all three Presidents of the Southern Baptist Convention (SBC) who presided over BFM Study Committees, and a recent doctrinal statement affirmed by a variety of Southern Baptist statesmen.

## A Baptist "Founder"

From Article 5 of "A Short Confession of Faith in Twenty Articles" by **John Smyth** (1570–1612): "That there is no original sin (lit., no sin of origin or descent), but all sin is actual and voluntary, viz., a word, a deed, or a design against the law of God; and therefore, infants are without sin."[23] John Smyth, an early Baptist "founder," clearly denies inherited guilt.

## 100 Years of Theology at SWBTS

Baptist theologian and historian James Leo Garrett Jr., in personal correspondence quoted with his permission, provides the following historical perspective: "Southern Seminary has had a wide divergence of views on your topic; for example, between Boyce and Dale Moody and between Dale Moody and Al Mohler. Southwestern Seminary, on the other hand, has consistently been on one side, i.e., we are not guilty of Adam's sin. **Walter T. Conner** repeatedly took this stance." After citing examples to support this claim,[24] Garrett explains: "Conner was the theology department at SWBTS from 1910 to 1949. I have known, I believe, every person who has taught theology as a full faculty member since 1949, and I cannot identify any one of these who taught that we are all guilty of the sin of Adam (and Eve), with one possible exception."[25] It is the testimony of Dr. Garrett that for over 100 years the theology faculty at SWBTS has affirmed: we are not guilty of Adam's sin.

## SBC Presidents Who Presided Over BFM Study Committees

**E. Y. Mullins** *(1860–1928) served as President of The Southern Baptist Theological Seminary (1899–1928). He was also President of the SBC when the Baptist Faith and Message (BFM) was adopted as its first statement of faith in 1925. Mullins rejected the doctrine of inherited guilt. He argued that man is not guilty because of his nature. Also, man is not guilty because he was represented by Adam in the garden or because we were seminally present in Adam. Rather, man "is guilty when he does wrong." Adam's guilt is not imputed to humanity. Mullins explains, "Men are not condemned therefore for hereditary or original sin. They are condemned only for their own sins."[26]*

**Herschel Hobbs** *(1907–95) presided over the BFM 1963 Study Committee. In a 1979 article in which he describes the changes between the 1925 and 1963 editions of the BFM, Hobbs comments specifically on Article 3:*

> *Thus the result of the fall is that men inherit, not "a nature corrupt and in bondage to sin" (1925), but a "nature and an environment inclined toward sin" (1963). In the latter "condemnation" comes upon individuals following transgression "as soon as they are capable of moral action." This, of course, agrees with the position generally held by Baptists concerning God's grace in cases of those under the age of accountability and the mentally incompetent.[27]*

*Hobbs is clear: people do not inherit "a nature corrupt and in bondage to sin" (per the BFM 1925) but a nature "inclined toward sin." Also, condemnation follows transgression, which comes as soon as people are capable of moral action. Although it was possible to read inherited guilt into the BFM 1925, the 1963 revision made such a move nearly impossible. This was the view of the President of the SBC who convened the Study Committee which revised the BFM in 1963 (see Appendix A for the 1963 revision).*

*In 2000, **Paige Patterson** (b. 1942) served as President of the SBC when the BFM Study Committee recommended its most recent revision. It was unnecessary to scour Patterson's writings to ascertain his view of inherited guilt because he supervised my Ph.D. dissertation, which argues against it. After describing the method and goal in the foreword of my book, Patterson writes: "Harwood's conclusion that an infant is born with a sin nature, which makes the commission of rebellious acts inevitable, though the infant as yet carries no guilt, is not unusual or novel."[28] Patterson finds nothing "unusual or novel" about rejecting Adam's guilt and affirming a sinful nature.*

*Every SBC President who has presided over a BFM study committee has denied inherited guilt.*

### · A Recent Doctrinal Statement

*In 2012, after interacting with several Southern Baptist professors and pastors, Eric Hankins penned "A Statement of the Traditional Southern Baptist Understanding of God's Plan of Salvation." One line states: "We deny that Adam's sin resulted in the incapacitation of any person's free will or rendered any person guilty before he has personally sinned."[28] Prior to its release, a host of Southern Baptist statesmen affirmed it by publicly attaching their name and reputation, including: former SBC Presidents, current SBC Seminary Presidents, members of the BFM 2000 Study Committee, state executive–directors, and a variety of SBC pastors and professors. The affirmation of the Traditional Statement by these leaders is not an argument for or against its content. But their affirmation supports the claim that many Southern Baptists hold this view: we're not guilty of Adam's sin.*

*The list of theologians from Christian and Baptist history who are comfortable ignoring or denying inherited guilt is impressive. If the accusation of Pelagianism is once again wrongly leveled against the view (as it was against Zwingli and Marpeck), then I'll be in good company.*

## Objection: What about the Imputation of Christ's Righteousness?

*Calvinistic brothers in the SBC sometimes object: Isn't the imputation of Christ's righteousness a response to the imputation of Adam's guilt? My reply: No. What does the Bible teach us about the righteousness of God? Romans 3:21–22 states: "The righteousness of God has been manifested apart from the law, although the Law and the Prophets bear witness to it—the righteousness of God through faith in Jesus Christ for all who believe." 3:28: "For we hold that one is justified by faith apart from the works of the law." Consider 4:5: "And to the one who does not work but believes in him who justifies the ungodly, his faith is counted as righteousness..."*

*Abraham believed God was able to do what He promised. Consider Rom 4:22–25: "That is why his faith was counted to him as righteousness. But the words 'it was counted to him' were not written for his sake alone, but for ours also. It will be counted to us who believe in him who raised from the dead Jesus our Lord, who was delivered up for our trespasses and raised for our justification." Paul's point in Romans 3 and 4 is that others are made righteous in the same way as Abraham — by faith.*

*In the Bible, faith being counted by God as righteousness doesn't require an imputation of Adam's guilt. It requires believing in Jesus.*

## Why This Matters for Southern Baptists

*Some of you may not see a problem. You might say, "Christians differ on many issues." True. But now Southern Baptists differ. Some teach that Adam alone is guilty of Adam's sin. Others teach that the guilt of Adam's sin falls on everyone. Consider, for example, the differences between Article 3 of the BFM and a Southern Baptist Theological Seminary (SBTS) document entitled "An Exposition from the Faculty of The Southern Baptist Theological Seminary on The Baptist Faith and Message 2000."[29]*

| Article 3 of the BFM (see Appendix A for full article) | SBTS Faculty Exposition of Article 3 |
|---|---|
| Through the temptation of Satan man transgressed the command of God, and fell from his original innocence whereby his posterity inherit a nature and an environment inclined toward sin. Therefore, as soon as they are capable of moral action, they become transgressors and under condemnation. | In accordance with the biblical perspective of the entire human race as united in descent from Adam, the guilt of Adam's sin falls on all, and estrangement from God in whose image we are made extends to all. |

Notice the BFM states all people (Adam's "posterity") "inherit a nature and an environment inclined toward sin." What do we inherit from Adam? According to the BFM, people inherit "a nature and an environment inclined toward sin." When are people under condemnation? "As soon as they are capable of moral action, they become transgressors and under condemnation."

But the SBTS faculty exposition of the BFM affirms a view not found in the BFM. The faculty exposition makes no mention of: a nature inclined toward sin, becoming capable of moral action, or becoming transgressors. Instead, it reads: "In accordance with the biblical perspective of the entire human race as united in descent from Adam, the guilt of Adam's sin falls on all, and estrangement from God in whose image we are made extends to all." According to the SBTS faculty exposition of the BFM, people begin life "estranged from God." Why? Because "the guilt of Adam's sin falls on all." All people begin life guilty because of Adam's sin.

I don't mean to imply by contrasting the BFM with the SBTS faculty exposition that the SBTS faculty do not affirm the BFM. But the faculty exposition omits concepts found in the BFM and replaces them with a theological viewpoint not found in the BFM, namely that people all people are guilty of Adam's sin.

Southern Baptists who affirm different views on Adam's guilt can and should cooperate in the work of the Great Commission. One reason I am addressing this issue publicly is to foster understanding within the SBC and to suggest these are orthodox but differing views. Both views of guilt are permissible within the evangelical world. But it seems necessary that if SBC seminaries publish interpretations of the BFM, then such interpretations must accurately reflect the BFM.

A primary—but not universal—commitment among Calvinistic brothers is that all people begin life guilty and condemned, accountable to God due to the sin and guilt of Adam. Historically, Calvinists become unsettled when inherited guilt is denied. I have no desire to unsettle my brothers in Christ. But, inherited guilt is not affirmed in the BFM. I regard inherited guilt to be both unnecessary and unhelpful for interpreting the Bible. Even so, I have said repeatedly their view is orthodox. Yet I have been accused of wanting to "push" people out of the SBC and my view has been labeled by some as dangerous and heretical.

My desire is for unity. I consider this to be a family discussion of theological differences among brothers and sisters in Christ, co-laborers in Great Commission work. I plan to regard any rebuttals of this presentation as critiques from believers who share my desire to be faithful to God and to His Word.

One might still insist: "Why are you making such a big deal about this? We're guilty of our own sin—or Adam's sin. Why does it matter? Either way, we're all sinners in need of a savior." Here's the big deal: Romans 5:12-21 doesn't say we're guilty of Adam's sin. Search your Bible. No Bible verse states that other people are guilty of Adam's sin. And I am unwilling to say more than God reveals clearly in His Word regarding Adam's sin and the timing of personal accountability and guilt. If we are not guilty of Adam's sin, then a primary commitment of Calvinism is rendered unnecessary for sound biblical theology.

# End Notes

1   For the use of "inclined toward sin," see Article 3 of the BFM; for "orig-
    inal death" rather than "original sin," see James D. G. Dunn, *Romans
    1–8* in WBC, vol. 38A (Dallas: Word, 1988), 273, and Douglas Moo,
    Romans in NICNT (Grand Rapids: Eerdmans, 1996), 322–323.

2   For a full treatment of this subject, see my book *The Spiritual Condition
    of Infants: A Biblical–Historical Survey and Systematic Proposal* (Eu-
    gene, OR: Wipf & Stock, 2011). My book is actually a popular version
    of my doctoral dissertation for which I received a Ph.D. in Theology
    from Southwestern Baptist Theological Seminary.

3   Wayne Grudem, *Systematic Theology* (Grand Rapids: Zondervan,
    1994), 494–495. The subsection describing his view is entitled "In-
    herited Guilt: We Are Counted Guilty Because of Adam's Sin." While
    Grudem embraces Covenant Theology so far as the present subject is
    concerned, he remains a Calvinistic Baptist.

4   N. T. Wright, "The Letter to the Romans" in *The New Interpreter's
    Bible*, vol. X (Nashville: Abingdon, 2002), 523.

5   Unless otherwise noted, the English Standard Version will be used.

6   Jospeh Fitzmyer, *Romans* in The Anchor Bible, vol. 33 (Garden City,
    NY: Doubleday, 1993), 411.

7   Barclay M. Newman and Eugene A. Nida, *A Translator's Handbook on
    Paul's Letter to the Romans* (New York: United Bible Societies, 1973).
    Electronic edition via Translator's Workplace 4.0.

8   For more on Augustine's use of a poor translation of eph' hō in Rom
    5:12, see David Weaver, "From Paul to Augustine: Romans 5:12 in Early
    Christian Exegesis," St. Vladimir's Theological Quarterly 27 (1983):
    187–206; and Frank J. Matera, *Romans* in PCNT (Grand Rapids: Baker
    Academic, 2010), 126.

9   Fitzmyer, Romans, 408–409.

10  See Peter J. Gentry and Stephen Wellum, *Kingdom Through Covenant:
    A Biblical–Theological Understanding of Covenants* (Wheaton: Cross-
    way, 2012), 59–62; Michael Horton, *God of Promise: Introducing
    Covenantal Theology* (Grand Rapids: Baker, 2006), 77–110; and John
    Murray, "Covenant Theology" in *Collected Works*, vol. 4 (Carlisle, PA:
    Banner of Truth, 1982), 216–240.

11 J. W. MacGorman, *Romans: Everyman's Gospel* (Nashville: Convention Press, 1976), 79. Thanks to Peter Lumpkins for bringing this reference to my attention.

12 Millard J. Erickson, *Christian Theology*, 2d ed. (Grand Rapids: Baker, 1998), 656. Erickson's view is typically dismissed by Calvinistic brothers; understandably so, because Erickson writes that "the biblical evidence favors the position that conversion is prior to regeneration" (945).

13 Emphasis added.

14 Transcript is from John Piper, "What Happens to Infants Who Die?" http://www.desiringgod.org/resource-library/ask-pastor-john/what-hap-pens-to-infants-who-die--2 (accessed January 14, 2013).

15 John Piper, *Jesus: The Only Way to God: Must You Hear the Gospel to be Saved?* (Grand Rapids: Baker, 2010), 77 n. 6. Surprisingly, Piper cites in support of his claim Ronald Nash, *When a Baby Dies* (Grand Rapids: Zondervan, 1999), who argues in chapter 3 against precisely the view to which Piper is open, salvation via post-mortem faith.

16 Stan Norman, "Human Sinfulness," in *A Theology for the Church* (Nashville: B&H Academic, 2007), 449.

17 John Chrysostom, *On Infants*, ed. and trans. Henry Bettenson, in The Later Christian Fathers (New York: Oxford University Press, 1971), 69.

18 Gregory of Nyssa, *On Infants' Early Deaths*, in NPNF2 5: 372–381.

19 See Tertullian, *A Treatise on the Soul* 39–41, 56, in ANF 3:219–221, 232; and On Baptism 18 in ANF 3:678.

20 Eric Osborn, Tertullian, *First Theologian of the West* (Cambridge: Cambridge University Press, 1997), 167.

21 Ulrich Zwingli, *On Original Sin, in On Providence and Other Essays*, trans. Samuel Jackson (Durham, NC: Labyrinth Press, 1983), 3–10.

22 Pilgram Marpeck, *Response to Caspar Schwenckfeld's Judgment, in The Writings of Pilgram Marpeck*, ed. and trans. Walter Klaassen and William Klaassen, in CRR, vol. 2 (Scottsdale, PA: Herald Press, 1978), 89.

23 "A Short Confession of Faith in Twenty Articles by John Smyth," http://www.baptistcenter.com/baptist_confessions/general_baptist/A-Short-Confession-of-Faith-in-Twenty-Articles.html (accessed January 24, 2013).

24  See W. T. Conner, *The Faith of the New Testament* (Nashville: Broadman, 1940), 286–289; *A System of Christian Doctrine* (1924); and the revision of its second half, *The Gospel of Redemption* (1945).

25  James Leo Garrett, Jr., in correspondence to the author dated January 22, 2013.

26  E. Y. Mullins, *The Christian Religion in Its Doctrinal Expression* (Valley Forge, PA: Judson Press, 1917; reprinted 1974), 302.

27  Herschel H. Hobbs, "Southern Baptists and Confessionalism: A Comparison of the Origins and Contents of the 1925 and 1963 Confessions," Review and Expositor 76.1 (1979): 63. I am indebted to Peter Lumpkins, who drew my attention to this journal article.

28  Paige Patterson, "Foreword" to Harwood, *The Spiritual Condition of Infants*, ix.

29  See http://sbctoday.com/wp-content/uploads/2012/06/A-Statement-of-Traditional-Southern-Baptist-Soteriology-SBC-Today.pdf (accessed January 24, 2013). Quote is from Article 2.

30  See http://www.sbts.edu/resources/booklets/an-exposition-from-the-faculty-of-the-southern-baptist-theological-seminary-on-the-baptist-faith-and-message-2000/ (accessed January 18, 2013).

# Appendix A

*At right are three versions of one article on the sinful human condition taken from three editions of The Baptist Faith and Message (BFM), the sole confession of faith ever to be endorsed by The Southern Baptist Convention. Southern Baptists first adopted the BFM in 1925 and subsequently passed two revisions—1963 and 2000. See http://sbc.net/bfm/bfm-comparison.asp (accessed January 30, 2013). The articles lack biblical references. Interested inquirers may view all three versions of the entire confession complete with biblical references at the website address above.*

## III. The Fall of Man (1925)

Man was created by the special act of God, as recorded in Genesis. "So God created man in his own image, in the image of God created he him; male and female created he them" (Gen. 1:27). "And the Lord God formed man of the dust of the ground, and breathed into his nostrils the breath of life; and man became a living soul" (Gen. 2:7).

He was created in a state of holiness under the law of his Maker, but, through the temptation of Satan, he transgressed the command of God and fell from his original holiness and righteousness; whereby his posterity inherit a nature corrupt and in bondage to sin, are under condemnation, and as soon as they are capable of moral action, become actual transgressors.

| III. Man (1963) | III. Man (2000) |
|---|---|
| Man was created by the special act of God, in His own image, and is the crowning work of His creation. In the beginning man was innocent of sin and was endowed by his Creator with freedom of choice. By his free choice man sinned against God and brought sin into the human race. Through the temptation of Satan man transgressed the command of God, and fell from his original innocence; whereby his posterity inherit a nature and an environment inclined toward sin, and as soon as they are capable of moral action become transgressors and are under condemnation. Only the grace of God can bring man into His holy fellowship and enable man to fulfil the creative purpose of God. The sacredness of human personality is evident in that God created man in His own image, and in that Christ died for man; therefore every man possesses dignity and is worthy of respect and Christian love. | Man is the special creation of God, made in His own image. He created them male and female as the crowning work of His creation. The gift of gender is thus part of the goodness of God's creation. In the beginning man was innocent of sin and was endowed by his Creator with freedom of choice. By his free choice man sinned against God and brought sin into the human race. Through the temptation of Satan man transgressed the command of God, and fell from his original innocence whereby his posterity inherit a nature and an environment inclined toward sin. Therefore, as soon as they are capable of moral action, they become transgressors and are under condemnation. Only the grace of God can bring man into His holy fellowship and enable man to fulfill the creative purpose of God. The sacredness of human personality is evident in that God created man in His own image, and in that Christ died for man; therefore, every person of every race possesses full dignity and is worthy of respect and Christian love. |

# Born Guilty?

# Appendix B

## A Statement of the Traditional Southern Baptist Understanding of God's Plan of Salvation

### Articles of Affirmation and Denial

### *Article One: The Gospel*

**We affirm** that the Gospel is the good news that God has made a way of salvation through the life, death, and resurrection of the Lord Jesus Christ for any person. This is in keeping with God's desire for every person to be saved.

**We deny** that only a select few are capable of responding to the Gospel while the rest are predestined to an eternity in hell.

### *Article Two: The Sinfulness of Man*

**We affirm** that, because of the fall of Adam, every person inherits a nature and environment inclined toward sin and that every person who is capable of moral action will sin. Each person's sin alone brings the wrath of a holy God, broken fellowship with Him, ever-worsening selfishness and destructiveness, death, and condemnation to an eternity in hell.

**We deny** that Adam's sin resulted in the incapacitation of any person's free will or rendered any person guilty before he has personally sinned. While no sinner is remotely capable of achieving salvation through his own effort, we deny that any sinner is saved apart from a free response to the Holy Spirit's drawing through the Gospel.

### *Article Three: The Atonement of Christ*

**We affirm** that the penal substitution of Christ is the only available and effective sacrifice for the sins of every person.

**We deny** that this atonement results in salvation without a person's free response of repentance and faith. We deny that God imposes or withholds this atonement without respect to an act of the person's free will. We deny that Christ died only for the sins of those who will be saved.

### Article Four: The Grace of God

**We affirm** that grace is God's generous decision to provide salvation for any person by taking all of the initiative in providing atonement, in freely offering the Gospel in the power of the Holy Spirit, and in uniting the believer to Christ through the Holy Spirit by faith.

**We deny** that grace negates the necessity of a free response of faith or that it cannot be resisted. We deny that the response of faith is in any way a meritorious work that earns salvation.

### Article Five: The Regeneration of the Sinner

**We affirm** that any person who responds to the Gospel with repentance and faith is born again through the power of the Holy Spirit. He is a new creation in Christ and enters, at the moment he believes, into eternal life.

**We deny** that any person is regenerated prior to or apart from hearing and responding to the Gospel.

### Article Six: The Election to Salvation

**We affirm** that, in reference to salvation, election speaks of God's eternal, gracious, and certain plan in Christ to have a people who are His by repentance and faith.

**We deny** that election means that, from eternity, God predestined certain people for salvation and others for condemnation.

### Article Seven: The Sovereignty of God

**We affirm** God's eternal knowledge of and sovereignty over every person's salvation or condemnation.

**We deny** that God's sovereignty and knowledge require Him to cause a person's acceptance or rejection of faith in Christ.

## Article Eight: The Free Will of Man

*We affirm that God, as an expression of His sovereignty, endows each person with actual free will (the ability to choose between two options), which must be exercised in accepting or rejecting God's gracious call to salvation by the Holy Spirit through the Gospel.*

*We deny that the decision of faith is an act of God rather than a response of the person. We deny that there is an "effectual call" for certain people that is different from a "general call" to any person who hears and understands the Gospel.*

## Article Nine: The Security of the Believer

*We affirm that when a person responds in faith to the Gospel, God promises to complete the process of salvation in the believer into eternity. This process begins with justification, whereby the sinner is immediately acquitted of all sin and granted peace with God; continues in sanctification, whereby the saved are progressively conformed to the image of Christ by the indwelling Holy Spirit; and concludes in glorification, whereby the saint enjoys life with Christ in heaven forever.*

*We deny that this Holy Spirit-sealed relationship can ever be broken. We deny even the possibility of apostasy.*

## Article Ten: The Great Commission

*We affirm that the Lord Jesus Christ commissioned His church to preach the good news of salvation to all people to the ends of the earth. We affirm that the proclamation of the Gospel is God's means of bringing any person to salvation.*

*We deny that salvation is possible outside of a faith response to the Gospel of Jesus Christ.*

1   See http://sbctoday.com/wp-content/uploads/2012/06/A-Statement-of-Traditional-Southern-Baptist-Soteriology-SBC-Today.pdf (accessed February 1, 2013). Used by Permission from Dr. Eric Hankins, Pastor of First Baptist Church, Oxford, Mississippi. Dr. Hankins' Introduction to the Traditional Statement, the Preamble, and the biblical references for each article are omitted above. Interested inquirers may obtain all three at www.sbctoday.com

# For further reading, consider Dr. Adam Harwood's book!

The Spiritual Condition of Infants: A Biblical-Historical Survey and Systematic Proposal *by Adam Harwood. Published by Wipf & Stock Publishers (2011), Dr. Harwood examines several biblical texts and compares his findings with the writings of over a dozen theologians. According to the Augustinian-Calvinist view, all people inherit from the first Adam both a sinful nature and his guilt. If they are correct, then all infants are subject to the judgment of God against their nature before they knowingly commit any sinful actions. Is this what Scripture clearly teaches? His quest is to clarify the spiritual condition of infants and separate what the Bible actually says from what many theologians have deduced from their theological reasoning.*

(order from Wipf & Stock Publishers and amazon.com)

"Through extensively examining relevant biblical and historical sources, two major questions with profound pastoral consequences are answered in this important book: Do infants inherit a sin nature from Adam? Although utilizing different models, most theologians agree that infants inherit a sin nature. However, are infants, therefore, guilty before God? In answering this second question, Adam Harwood challenges the dominant systematic discourse and properly reorients our understanding of infant salvation. Harwood's careful thesis will stand." —**Malcolm B. Yarnell III**, Associate Professor of Systematic Theology Southwestern Baptist Theological Seminary, Fort Worth, TX

"Dr. Harwood has written a wonderful book that will be of great benefit to the academic world as scholars struggle with the theoretical implications of the issue of infants and salvation, but more importantly, it will be of greater benefit to those who not only struggle with the theoretical issue, but are on the front lines ministering to grieving people who have lost beloved infants. This book lays out in a clear, intelligent, and accessible manner the issues surrounding the eternal destiny of those who die in infancy. Dr. Harwood is to be commended for his work." —**Rustin J. Umstattd**, Associate Academic Dean and Assistant Professor of Theology Midwestern Baptist Theological Seminary, Kansas City, MO

(Reviews taken from the publisher's website, www.wipfandstock.com)

## Other Books by Free Church Press

(Available through freechurchpress.com, amazon.com)

**Urgent: Igniting a Passion for Jesus,** *by Joe Donahue; Foreword by Ergun Caner. A personal story that many teens find themselves in today.*

**Ancient Wine and the Bible: The Case for Abstinence,** *by David R. Brumbelow; Foreword by Paige Patterson. Detailed study of wine, Scripture, and reasons for abstinence.*

**Green Pastures of a Barren Land: finding contentment in life's desolate seasons** *by Candise Farmer. After the Foreword by Kay Arthur, Candise offers biblical encouragement to those facing difficult moments in life. In addition, Candise offers an inductive Bible study for small groups as a supplement to her book.*

**A Journey Through the Bible: From Genesis to Malachi,** *by Jerry Vines. Volume I. Introduction, outline, and synopsis of each Old Testament book by one of America's leading expositors.*

**A Journey Through the Bible: From Matthew to Revelation,** *by Jerry Vines. Volume II. Introduction, outline, and synopsis of each New Testament book.*

**All the Days: Daily Devotions for Busy Believers** *by Jerry Vines. An inspiring devotion for each day of the week.*

**A Gentle Zephyr-A Mighty Wind: Silhouettes of life in the Spirit** *by J. Gerald Harris. The longtime editor of a Christian paper, Harris writes a fresh exploration of the biblical doctrine of the Holy Spirit and does so in a way that church members can both read and grasp without sacrificing scholarly integrity.*

**Straight Shooting: Pastoral Reflections for Today's Church** *by William "Bill" Harrell. A veteran pastor takes an honest look at the moral corruption of our culture and the church's unfortunate failure to stop it.*

## Other books of note:

**Alcohol Today: Abstinence in an Age of Indulgence**, *by Peter Lumpkins; Foreword by Jerry Vines. Published in 2009 by Hannibal Books, a devastating argument against the use of a mind-altering drug. (order through alcoholtoday.com, and amazon.com)*

**Whosoever Will: A Biblical-Theological Critique of Five-Point Calvinism** *edited by David L. Allen and Steve W. Lemke. Published by B&H Academic, this volume remains the definitive challenge to the neo-Calvinist Resurgence in evangelicalism generally and within the Southern Baptist Convention particularly. (order from amazon.com and Lifeway Christian Resources)*

CPSIA information can be obtained at www.ICGtesting.com
Printed in the USA
LVOW05s003505021 4
372315LV00003B/90/P